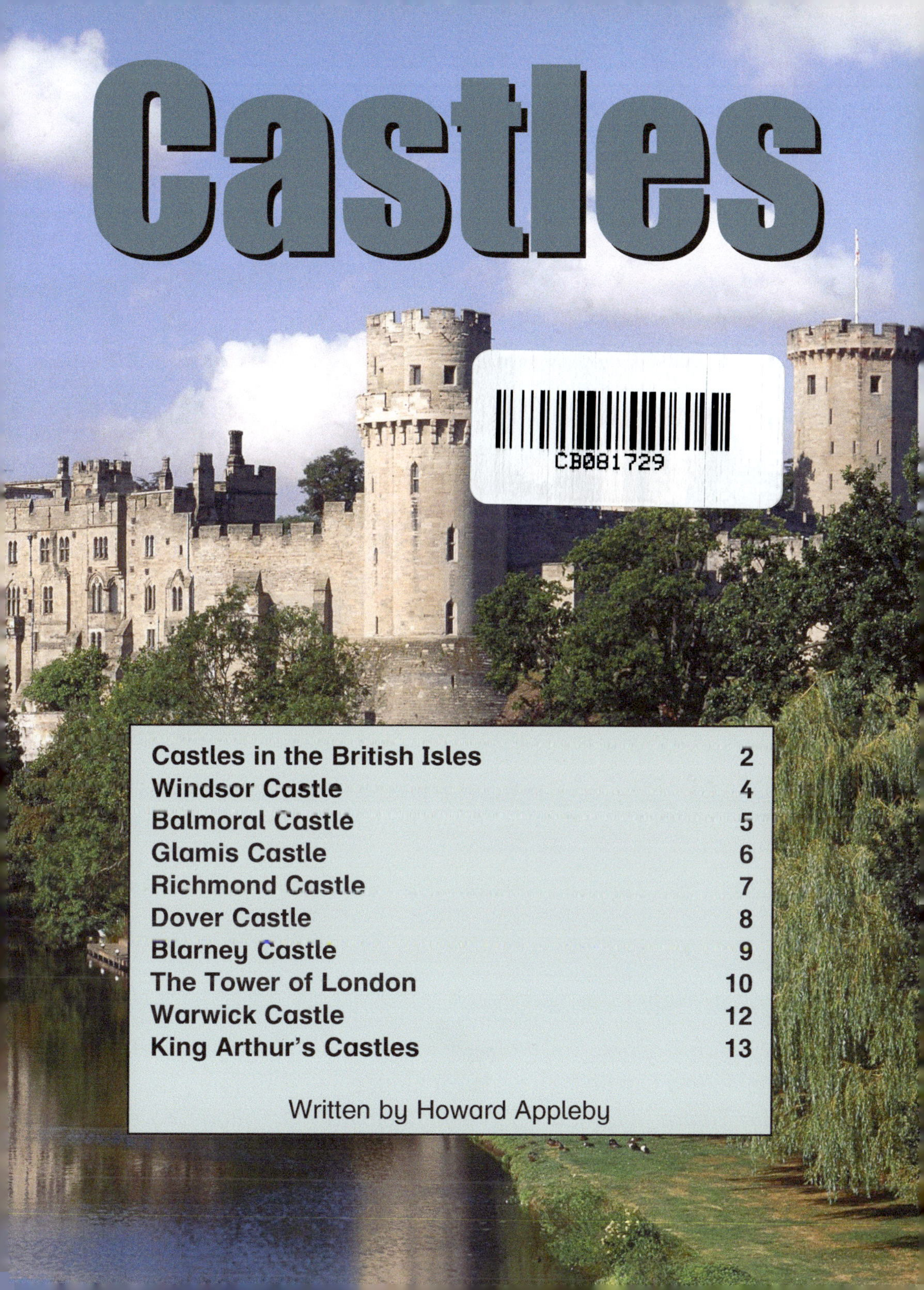

Castles

Written by Howard Appleby

There are hundreds of castles in the British Isles. Some of them are ruins, but others are in very good condition. Some castles are homes for famous people like the King of England! Many of them are very, very old and have got a fascinating history.

Castles in the British Isles

Key

1 Windsor Castle
2 Balmoral Castle
3 Glamis Castle
4 Richmond Castle
5 Dover Castle
6 Blarney Castle
7 The Tower of London
8 Warwick Castle
9 Tintagel Castle
10 Cadbury Castle

Castles are big, strong buildings. People built castles in the past to protect everyone inside the castle from attack.

Many castles have legends. Legends are stories about people and places in the past. There are legends of ghosts, wizards, kings and queens, and heroes. Read about some of these in the next few pages.

A castle under attack

Windsor Castle

Windsor Castle is one of the places where the King of England lives. It is the biggest inhabited castle in the world.

William the Conqueror (1028–1087) invaded England in 1066 and built this castle. It is 45 kilometres west of London.

The castle is full of treasures and famous paintings. But it is also full of ghosts of kings and queens who lived here many years ago. In the Royal Library you can hear footsteps. They are the footsteps of the ghost of Queen Elizabeth I! She lived here in the 16th century.

In 1992, there was a big fire in Windsor Castle and it destroyed many of the treasures. The castle closed for a long time, but it is now open again for visitors. Visit the Great Hall! It is very beautiful.

Balmoral Castle

Balmoral Castle is another of the King of England's castles. The royal family usually go to Balmoral for Christmas.

Balmoral Castle was a present from Prince Albert to his wife, Queen Victoria. She was Queen of England from 1837 to 1901. She loved Scotland and Balmoral. Albert finished building the castle in 1856, so it is not a very old castle and there are no ghosts. The royal family can sleep in peace in Balmoral!

Balmoral Castle is in the north-east of Scotland.

Glamis Castle

Glamis Castle is in the east of Scotland near Dundee. It is over 600 years old and it has got a lot of beautiful tall towers.

Glamis Castle is a haunted castle. There are more than nine ghosts! One is Macbeth. He is the king in Shakespeare's famous play *Macbeth*. He murdered many people. There is also a ghost called the Grey Lady who lives in the castle chapel. Then there is the ghost of a lady with no tongue who runs through the castle gardens. And there is also a madman who walks on the roof at night!

Richmond Castle

Richmond Castle is in the north of England. It is over 900 years old. It is on a big hill next to a river. It has got two big towers. These are called *keeps*. It is the only castle in England with two keeps.

Soldiers lived in the castle in the First and Second World Wars. The castle was also a prison. Ghosts of the soldiers live in the secret tunnels under the castle.

You can visit the castle and climb up to the top of the keeps, but you cannot visit the secret tunnels.

The main keep of Richmond Castle

Dover Castle

Dover Castle is a very big, old castle in England. It is on the south-east coast of England. It is on top of the famous white cliffs of Dover.

The castle has got an extremely big keep. There are also hundreds of tunnels in the cliffs under the castle.

You can visit the castle and the secret tunnels, but don't worry – there are no ghosts here!

The keep at Dover Castle

Blarney Castle

Blarney Castle is a very old castle in Ireland. It is eight kilometres from Cork. The King of Munster built the castle in 1446.

Kissing the Stone of Eloquence

The castle is famous for the *Stone of Eloquence*. This is a magic stone. You kiss it, and then you can speak other languages very well. One kiss and you can speak English!

The Tower of London

The Tower of London is in the centre of London, next to the River Thames. It is over 900 years old and it was a famous prison and place of execution.

The Tower is full of the ghosts of past kings, queens, princes and princesses. They were all prisoners in the Tower *dungeons*. A dungeon is a prison under the ground.

The ghosts of two little princes and Queen Anne Boleyn, one of King Henry VIII's wives, haunt the Tower of London.

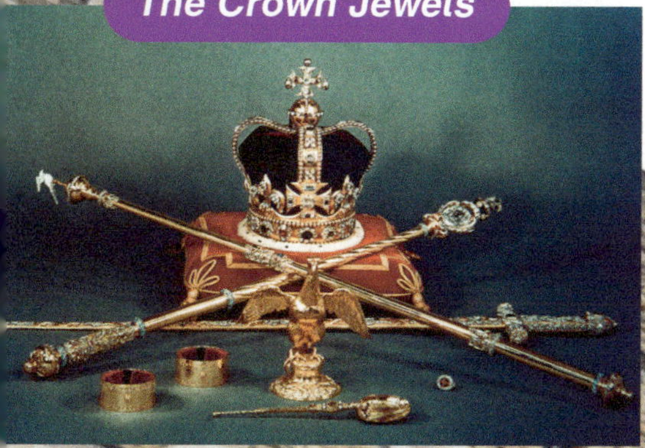

The Crown Jewels

There are guards at the Tower in special black and red uniforms. They are called Beefeaters. There are also a lot of big black birds called ravens.

The Crown Jewels are in a museum at the Tower of London and thousands of tourists queue to see them.

Warwick Castle

Warwick Castle is near Coventry in England. It is more than 600 years old and was the home of the Earl of Warwick.

Warwick Castle is famous for its towers and a keep that is a ruin. The names of the towers are Guy's Tower, Caesar's Tower and the Ghost Tower. Under Caesar's Tower is the cold and dark dungeon. Prisoners lived in this dungeon for years. There are messages on the walls from all the prisoners. You can still read them today. One message is from a prisoner in the 16th century!

You can visit the castle today, but there are no prisoners in the dungeon. However, there are lots of fun things to do and see.

King Arthur's Castles – Tintagel

Tintagel was a beautiful 12th-century stone castle. Today it is a ruin on the coast of south-west England with views over the sea.

Tintagel is famous for its legends of magic and mystery.

One legend says that Merlin the magician lived in Tintagel. There is a tunnel under the castle. This is called Merlin's Cave. The ghost of Merlin lives there and you can sometimes hear him talking. Is he saying magic spells?

Another legend says that King Arthur lived in Tintagel. In 1998 archeologists discovered a stone at Tintagel with the name ARTOGNOV on it. Artognov is Latin for the Celtic name Arthnou. Was Arthnou King Arthur?

King Arthur's Castles – Cadbury

Cadbury Castle is in the south-west of England. Some people believe this was the site for Arthur's famous castle, Camelot, where he lived with his wife, Queen Guinevere and the Knights of the Round Table.

King Arthur's Castles – Richmond

Another legend says that King Arthur is asleep in the tunnels under Richmond Castle. The legend says that King Arthur is asleep and waiting for the day that England needs him.

So where is King Arthur? Read the following story about Richmond Castle and find out.

King Arthur's Treasure

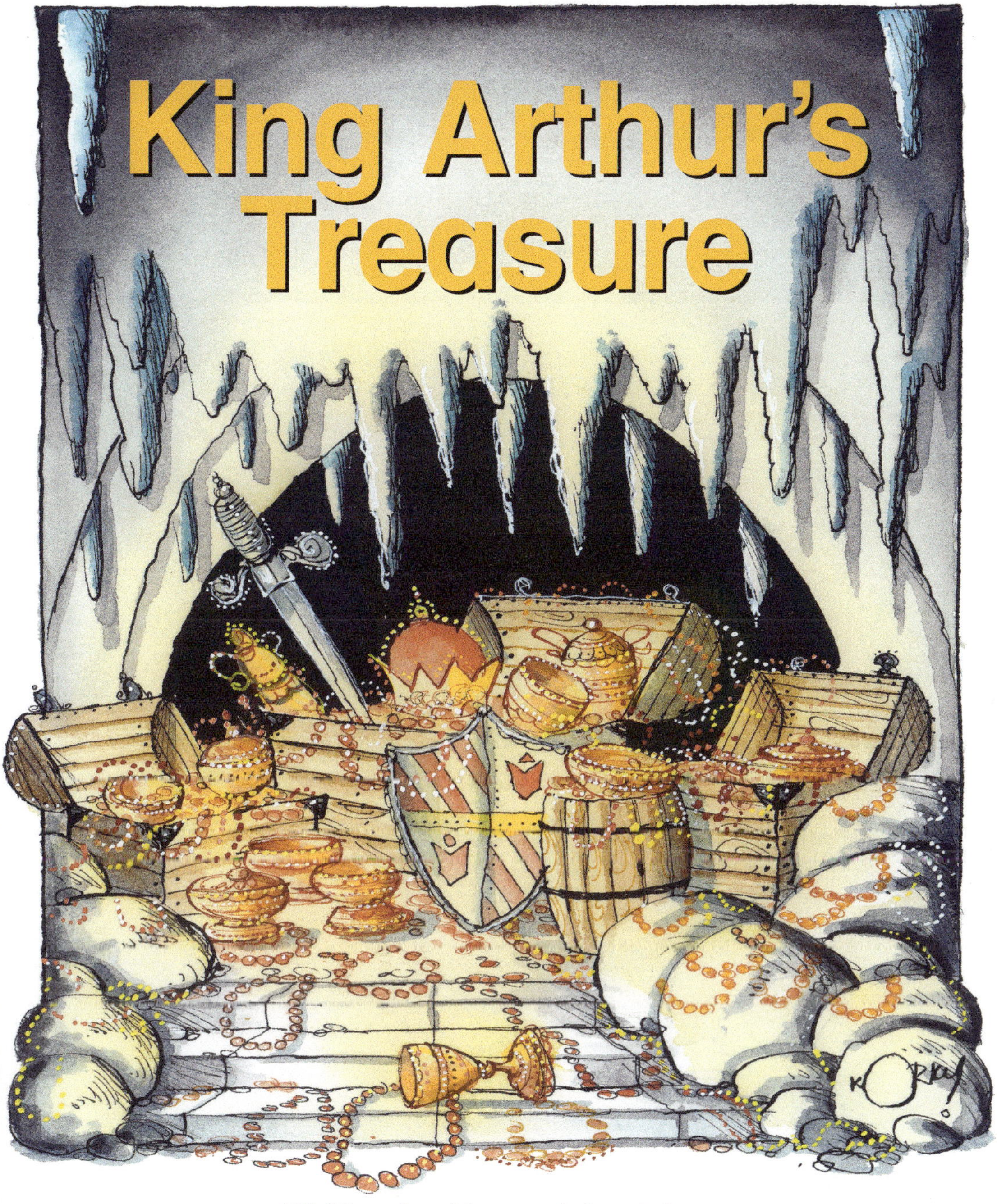

Written by Howard Appleby
Illustrated by Korky Paul

Peter Pitt was a shepherd in Richmond in the north of England. He watched the sheep on the hill next to the castle. There were nearly a hundred sheep!

One cold day in autumn an old man stopped Peter on the path. He was tall with a long white beard. He carried a long stick.

Peter Pitt was afraid. The old man was a wizard. Wizards are powerful. They know magic!

Merlin showed Peter his magic stick. Peter wanted to find the treasure.

There was an old apple tree near the castle. Peter walked to it with Merlin. Merlin moved the leaves on the ground around the tree. Peter saw a door. Merlin opened the door and Peter saw a tunnel going under the castle.

Peter followed Merlin into the tunnel. The magic stick was like a torch. The tunnel was long and dark. At the end of the tunnel there was an enormous cave.

At the entrance to the cave there was a big bell. There was a king asleep in the cave with a beautiful gold crown on his head. He was in silver armour with a big sword in his hand. Next to him there were many knights in armour with swords and shields. In the middle of the cave there was a huge pile of treasure.

Merlin explained to Peter that Arthur and the knights stay asleep until somebody rings the bell. Then they wake up and save England. He showed Peter a message on the wall.

Merlin pointed to the treasure on the floor.

Merlin turned, walked out of the cave and disappeared.

Peter Pitt filled his bag with gold and jewels from the cave and carried it outside. It was sunny and he was very happy.

So Peter Pitt returned to the cave and filled his bag again. The pile of gold outside the cave was bigger now but Peter wanted more gold. The third time he returned to the cave he bumped the bell with his head. It started to ring very loudly.

The Knights opened their eyes. They looked at Peter Pitt.

King Arthur was very, very angry now. England did not need him. It was a mistake.

Peter started to run. The knights followed him. He jumped out of the tunnel. The door of the tunnel closed behind him with a big crash.

Peter looked behind him. The door disappeared. He looked in his bag. It was full of stones! He looked at the ground. There was a big pile of stones and no treasure.

He looked for his sheep. There were no sheep on the hill.

Peter wasn't happy now. He was the poorest man in Richmond. He looked and looked under the old apple tree. Nothing was there!

And now nobody knows where King Arthur and the Knights of the Round Table are sleeping. Are they still waiting for the bell to ring?

Activities

1 Complete.

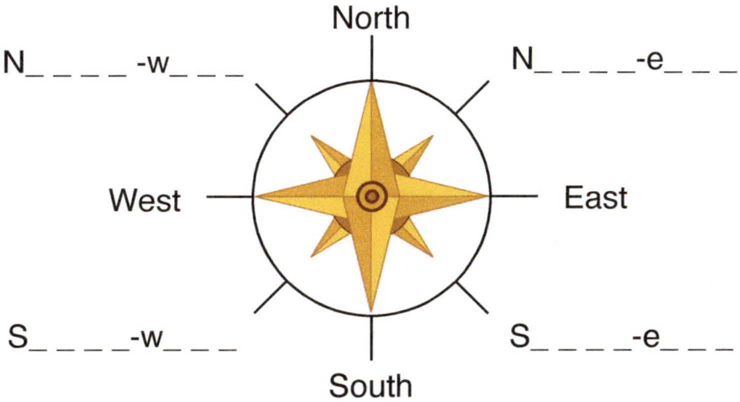

2 Match the castles to the sentences.

Balmoral	Tintagel	~~Glamis~~	The Tower of London	
Dover	Blarney	Windsor	Richmond	Warwick

1 This castle has got more than nine ghosts. ____Glamis____

2 This castle has got a magic stone. ________________

3 There was a big fire in this castle. ________________

4 Merlin's Cave is here. ________________

5 The royal family spend Christmas here. ________________

6 King Arthur is asleep in a tunnel under this castle. ________________

7 A castle on top of white chalk cliffs. ________________

8 There are beefeaters, ravens and crown jewels in this castle. ________________

9 This castle has a dungeon with messages from prisoners on the walls. ________________

3 Match the prepositions to the drawings.

near through in next to up

down on under around

4 Find these words in the word puzzle:

dungeon tower stone ghost knight cliff coast cave

d	p	t	o	w	e	r	p
u	c	a	l	a	c	e	k
n	f	c	a	v	e	k	n
g	h	o	s	t	s	n	i
e	v	a	g	h	t	i	g
o	f	s	y	u	o	o	h
n	m	t	s	k	n	o	t
c	l	i	f	f	e	q	k

5 Answer the questions and write about a castle in your country.

1 What is the name of your castle? ____________________
2 Where is it? ____________________
3 How old is it? ____________________
4 Who lived in the castle? ____________________
5 Who lives in the castle? ____________________
6 Has it got any towers? ____________________
7 Are there any ghosts? ____________________
8 Can you visit the castle? ____________________

(1) ____________ Castle is in (2) ____________ .
It is (3) ____________ old. (4) ____________ lived in the castle in the past. Nobody/(5) ____________ lives in the castle today. It has/hasn't got (6) ____________ . There are/aren't any (7) ____________ . You can/cannot (8) ____________ .

6 Look and write.

8 Put the sentences in the correct order.

Peter Pitt jumped out of the tunnel.	____
An old man stopped Peter Pitt on the path.	1
Peter Pitt filled his bag with gold and jewels.	____
Peter Pitt and Merlin looked under the apple tree for a tunnel.	____
The knights opened their eyes.	____
Peter Pitt was the richest man in Richmond.	____
Peter Pitt bumped his head on the bell.	____
Peter Pitt was the poorest man in Richmond.	____

9 Complete the story with the words in the box.

angry	tunnel	~~shepherd~~	head
stopped	filled	poorest	stones
wizard	bell	jumped	

Peter Pitt was a (1) *shepherd*. An old man (2) ____________ him on the path. The old man was a (3) ____________. He showed Peter Pitt the door to a (4) ____________. At the entrance of the cave there was a (5) ____________. Peter Pitt (6) ____________ his bag with gold and jewels from the cave. He bumped his (7) ____________ on the bell. The knights were (8) ____________. He (9) ____________ out of the tunnel. His bag was now full of (10) ____________. Peter Pitt was now the (11) ____________ man in Richmond.

Bilingual Dictionary

Write the words in your language.

armour	______	magic	______
attack	______	magician	______
bell	______	museum	______
build	______	prison	______
castle	______	queue	______
cave	______	raven	______
chapel	______	roof	______
cliff	______	royal	______
coast	______	ruin	______
crown	______	sheep	______
disappear	______	shepherd	______
dungeon	______	shield	______
footstep	______	site	______
ghost	______	soldier	______
gold	______	stone	______
guard	______	sword	______
haunted	______	tower	______
hill	______	treasure	______
invade	______	tunnel	______
jewel	______	war	______
knight	______	wizard	______
legend	______		

Macmillan Education
4 Crinan Street
London N1 9XW
A division of Springer Nature Limited
Companies and representatives throughout the world

ISBN 978-1-3800-3768-8

First published 2005
This edition published 2019

Illustrated by Korky Paul

The authors and publishers would like to thank the following for permission to reproduce their photographs:

Cover and title page images by Robert Harding Picture Library

Alamy Stock Photo/Granger Historical Picture Archive p11 (b), Collection Mix: Subjects/Charlie Harding p4, Alain le Casmeur p5, Michael Jenner p6, Roy Stedall-Humphrys p7, Alamy Stock Photo/Europe by Black Sea Images p9 (t), Robert Estall p10, Paul Watts p13 (t), Simon McBride p14 (t), Alamy Stock Photo/Mike Kipling Photography p14 (b), English Heritage Photo Library/ Jonathan Bailey p13 (b), Getty Images/Leon Neal p11 (c), Robert Harding Picture Library p8/12, Topham Picturepoint p11 (b); Alamy Stock Photo/Ken Welsh p9 (b).

Printed and bound in Brazil

2025
8